Six Months Planner

Plan your important moments in life

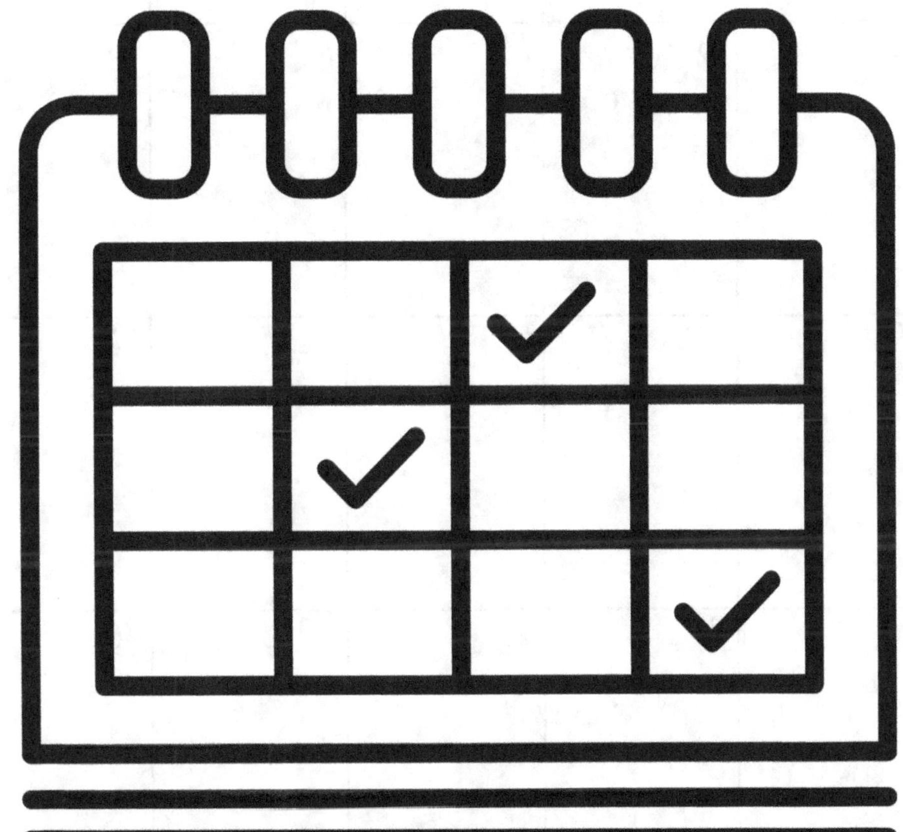

July 2021

Su	Mo	Tu	We	Th	Fr	Sa
				1	2	3
4	5	6	7	8	9	10
11	12	13	14	15	16	17
18	19	20	21	22	23	24
25	26	27	28	29	30	31
		Goals:				

July

Monday 28

Tuesday 29

Wednesday 30

Thursday 1

Friday 2

Saturday 3

Sunday 4

Goals:

July

Su	Mo	Tu	We	Th	Fr	Sa
				1	2	3
4	5	6	7	8	9	10
11	12	13	14	15	16	17
18	19	20	21	22	23	24
25	26	27	28	29	30	31

July

Monday 5

Tuesday 6

Wednesday 7

Thursday 8

Friday 9

Saturday 10

Sunday 11

Goals:

July

Su	Mo	Tu	We	Th	Fr	Sa
				1	2	3
4	5	6	7	8	9	10
11	12	13	14	15	16	17
18	19	20	21	22	23	24
25	26	27	28	29	30	31

July

Monday 12

Tuesday 13

Wednesday 14

Thursday 15

Friday 16

Saturday 17

Sunday 18

Goals:

July

Su	Mo	Tu	We	Th	Fr	Sa
				1	2	3
4	5	6	7	8	9	10
11	12	13	14	15	16	17
18	19	20	21	22	23	24
25	26	27	28	29	30	31

July

Monday 19

Tuesday 20

Wednesday 21

Thursday 22

Friday 23

Saturday 24

Sunday 25

Goals:

July

Su	Mo	Tu	We	Th	Fr	Sa
				1	2	3
4	5	6	7	8	9	10
11	12	13	14	15	16	17
18	19	20	21	22	23	24
25	26	27	28	29	30	31

July

<table>
<tr><td>Monday 26</td></tr>
<tr><td>

</td></tr>
<tr><td>Tuesday 27</td></tr>
<tr><td>

</td></tr>
<tr><td>Wednesday 28</td></tr>
<tr><td>

</td></tr>
<tr><td>Thursday 29</td></tr>
<tr><td>

</td></tr>
</table>

Friday 30

Saturday 31

Sunday 1

Goals:

July

Su	Mo	Tu	We	Th	Fr	Sa
				1	2	3
4	5	6	7	8	9	10
11	12	13	14	15	16	17
18	19	20	21	22	23	24
25	26	27	28	29	30	31

August 2021

Su	Mo	Tu	We	Th	Fr	Sa
1	2	3	4	5	6	7
8	9	10	11	12	13	14
15	16	17	18	19	20	21
22	23	24	25	26	27	28
29	30	31				

Goals:

August

Monday 26

Tuesday 27

Wednesday 28

Thursday 29

Friday 30

Saturday 31

Sunday 1

Goals:

August

Su	Mo	Tu	We	Th	Fr	Sa
1	2	3	4	5	6	7
8	9	10	11	12	13	14
15	16	17	18	19	20	21
22	23	24	25	26	27	28
29	30	31				

August

Monday 2

Tuesday 3

Wednesday 4

Thursday 5

Friday 6

Saturday 7

Sunday 8

Goals:

____

____

____

____

____

August

Su	Mo	Tu	We	Th	Fr	Sa
1	2	3	4	5	6	7
8	9	10	11	12	13	14
15	16	17	18	19	20	21
22	23	24	25	26	27	28
29	30	31				

August

Monday 9

Tuesday 10

Wednesday 11

Thursday 12

Friday 13

Saturday 14

Sunday 15

Goals:

August

Su	Mo	Tu	We	Th	Fr	Sa
1	2	3	4	5	6	7
8	9	10	11	12	13	14
15	16	17	18	19	20	21
22	23	24	25	26	27	28
29	30	31				

August

Monday 16

Tuesday 17

Wednesday 18

Thursday 19

Friday 20

Saturday 21

Sunday 22

Goals:

August

Su	Mo	Tu	We	Th	Fr	Sa
1	2	3	4	5	6	7
8	9	10	11	12	13	14
15	16	17	18	19	20	21
22	23	24	25	26	27	28
29	30	31				

August

<table>
<tr><td>Monday 23</td></tr>
<tr><td>Tuesday 24</td></tr>
<tr><td>Wednesday 25</td></tr>
<tr><td>Thursday 26</td></tr>
</table>

Friday 27

Saturday 28

Sunday 29

Goals:

____

____

____

____

____

August

Su	Mo	Tu	We	Th	Fr	Sa
1	2	3	4	5	6	7
8	9	10	11	12	13	14
15	16	17	18	19	20	21
22	23	24	25	26	27	28
29	30	31				

August

Monday 30

Tuesday 31

Wednesday 1

Thursday 2

Friday 3

Saturday 4

Sunday 5

Goals:

August

Su	Mo	Tu	We	Th	Fr	Sa
1	2	3	4	5	6	7
8	9	10	11	12	13	14
15	16	17	18	19	20	21
22	23	24	25	26	27	28
29	30	31				

September 2021

Su	Mo	Tu	We	Th	Fr	Sa
			1	2	3	4
5	6	7	8	9	10	11
12	13	14	15	16	17	18
19	20	21	22	23	24	25
26	27	28	29	30		

Goals:

September

Monday 30
Tuesday 31
Wednesday 1
Thursday 2

Friday 3

Saturday 4

Sunday 5

Goals:

September

Su	Mo	Tu	We	Th	Fr	Sa
			1	2	3	4
5	6	7	8	9	10	11
12	13	14	15	16	17	18
19	20	21	22	23	24	25
26	27	28	29	30		

September

Monday 6

Tuesday 7

Wednesday 8

Thursday 9

Friday 10

Saturday 11

Sunday 12

Goals:

September

Su	Mo	Tu	We	Th	Fr	Sa
			1	2	3	4
5	6	7	8	9	10	11
12	13	14	15	16	17	18
19	20	21	22	23	24	25
26	27	28	29	30		

September

Monday 13

Tuesday 14

Wednesday 15

Thursday 16

Friday 17

Saturday 18

Sunday 19

Goals:

____

____

____

____

____

September

Su	Mo	Tu	We	Th	Fr	Sa
			1	2	3	4
5	6	7	8	9	10	11
12	13	14	15	16	17	18
19	20	21	22	23	24	25
26	27	28	29	30		

September

Monday 20
Tuesday 21
Wednesday 22
Thursday 23

Friday 24

Saturday 25

Sunday 26

Goals:

____

____

____

____

____

September

Su	Mo	Tu	We	Th	Fr	Sa
			1	2	3	4
5	6	7	8	9	10	11
12	13	14	15	16	17	18
19	20	21	22	23	24	25
26	27	28	29	30		

September

Monday 27
Tuesday 28
Wednesday 29
Thursday 30

Friday 1

Saturday 2

Sunday 3

Goals:

____

____

____

____

____

September

Su	Mo	Tu	We	Th	Fr	Sa
			1	2	3	4
5	6	7	8	9	10	11
12	13	14	15	16	17	18
19	20	21	22	23	24	25
26	27	28	29	30		

October 2021

Su	Mo	Tu	We	Th	Fr	Sa
					1	2
3	4	5	6	7	8	9
10	11	12	13	14	15	16
17	18	19	20	21	22	23
24	25	26	27	28	29	30
31		Goals:				

October

<table>
<tr><td>Monday 27</td></tr>
<tr><td>Tuesday 28</td></tr>
<tr><td>Wednesday 29</td></tr>
<tr><td>Thursday 30</td></tr>
</table>

Friday 1

Saturday 2

Sunday 3

Goals: ____

____

____

____

____

October

Su	Mo	Tu	We	Th	Fr	Sa
					1	2
3	4	5	6	7	8	9
10	11	12	13	14	15	16
17	18	19	20	21	22	23
24	25	26	27	28	29	30
31						

October

<table>
<tr><td>Monday 4</td></tr>
<tr><td>Tuesday 5</td></tr>
<tr><td>Wednesday 6</td></tr>
<tr><td>Thursday 7</td></tr>
</table>

Friday 8

Saturday 9

Sunday 10

Goals:

October

Su	Mo	Tu	We	Th	Fr	Sa
					1	2
3	4	5	6	7	8	9
10	11	12	13	14	15	16
17	18	19	20	21	22	23
24	25	26	27	28	29	30
31						

October

Monday 11

Tuesday 12

Wednesday 13

Thursday 14

Friday 15

Saturday 16

Sunday 17

Goals:

October

Su	Mo	Tu	We	Th	Fr	Sa
					1	2
3	4	5	6	7	8	9
10	11	12	13	14	15	16
17	18	19	20	21	22	23
24	25	26	27	28	29	30
31						

October

Monday 18

Tuesday 19

Wednesday 20

Thursday 21

Friday 22

Saturday 23

Sunday 24

Goals:

____

____

____

____

____

October

Su	Mo	Tu	We	Th	Fr	Sa
					1	2
3	4	5	6	7	8	9
10	11	12	13	14	15	16
17	18	19	20	21	22	23
24	25	26	27	28	29	30
31						

October

Monday 25

Tuesday 26

Wednesday 27

Thursday 28

2021

Friday 29

Saturday 30

Sunday 31

Goals: _______________________________________

____

____

____

____

____

October

Su	Mo	Tu	We	Th	Fr	Sa
					1	2
3	4	5	6	7	8	9
10	11	12	13	14	15	16
17	18	19	20	21	22	23
24	25	26	27	28	29	30
31						

November 2021

Su	Mo	Tu	We	Th	Fr	Sa
	1	2	3	4	5	6
7	8	9	10	11	12	13
14	15	16	17	18	19	20
21	22	23	24	25	26	27
28	29	30				

Goals:

November

Monday 1

Tuesday 2

Wednesday 3

Thursday 4

Friday 5

Saturday 6

Sunday 7

Goals:

November

Su	Mo	Tu	We	Th	Fr	Sa
	1	2	3	4	5	6
7	8	9	10	11	12	13
14	15	16	17	18	19	20
21	22	23	24	25	26	27
28	29	30				

November

Monday 8

Tuesday 9

Wednesday 10

Thursday 11

Friday 12

Saturday 13

Sunday 14

Goals:

____

____

____

____

____

November

Su	Mo	Tu	We	Th	Fr	Sa
	1	2	3	4	5	6
7	8	9	10	11	12	13
14	15	16	17	18	19	20
21	22	23	24	25	26	27
28	29	30				

November

Monday 15

Tuesday 16

Wednesday 17

Thursday 18

Friday 19

Saturday 20

Sunday 21

Goals:

November

Su	Mo	Tu	We	Th	Fr	Sa
	1	2	3	4	5	6
7	8	9	10	11	12	13
14	15	16	17	18	19	20
21	22	23	24	25	26	27
28	29	30				

November

<table>
<tr><td>Monday 22</td></tr>
<tr><td>Tuesday 23</td></tr>
<tr><td>Wednesday 24</td></tr>
<tr><td>Thursday 25</td></tr>
</table>

Friday 26

Saturday 27

Sunday 28

Goals:

____

____

____

____

____

November

Su	Mo	Tu	We	Th	Fr	Sa
	1	2	3	4	5	6
7	8	9	10	11	12	13
14	15	16	17	18	19	20
21	22	23	24	25	26	27
28	29	30				

November

Monday 29
Tuesday 30
Wednesday 1
Thursday 2

Friday 3

Saturday 4

Sunday 5

Goals:

November

Su	Mo	Tu	We	Th	Fr	Sa
	1	2	3	4	5	6
7	8	9	10	11	12	13
14	15	16	17	18	19	20
21	22	23	24	25	26	27
28	29	30				

December 2021

Su	Mo	Tu	We	Th	Fr	Sa
			1	2	3	4
5	6	7	8	9	10	11
12	13	14	15	16	17	18
19	20	21	22	23	24	25
26	27	28	29	30	31	

Goals:

December

Monday 29

Tuesday 30

Wednesday 1

Thursday 2

Friday 3

Saturday 4

Sunday 5

Goals:

____

____

____

____

____

December

Su	Mo	Tu	We	Th	Fr	Sa
			1	2	3	4
5	6	7	8	9	10	11
12	13	14	15	16	17	18
19	20	21	22	23	24	25
26	27	28	29	30	31	

December

<table>
<tr><td>Monday 6</td></tr>
<tr><td>Tuesday 7</td></tr>
<tr><td>Wednesday 8</td></tr>
<tr><td>Thursday 9</td></tr>
</table>

Friday 10

Saturday 11

Sunday 12

Goals:

December

Su	Mo	Tu	We	Th	Fr	Sa
			1	2	3	4
5	6	7	8	9	10	11
12	13	14	15	16	17	18
19	20	21	22	23	24	25
26	27	28	29	30	31	

December

<table>
<tr><td>Monday 13</td></tr>
</table>

Tuesday 14

Wednesday 15

Thursday 16

Friday 17

Saturday 18

Sunday 19

Goals:

December

Su	Mo	Tu	We	Th	Fr	Sa
			1	2	3	4
5	6	7	8	9	10	11
12	13	14	15	16	17	18
19	20	21	22	23	24	25
26	27	28	29	30	31	

December

Monday 20

Tuesday 21

Wednesday 22

Thursday 23

Friday 24

Saturday 25

Sunday 26

Goals:

____

____

____

____

____

December

Su	Mo	Tu	We	Th	Fr	Sa
			1	2	3	4
5	6	7	8	9	10	11
12	13	14	15	16	17	18
19	20	21	22	23	24	25
26	27	28	29	30	31	

December

<table>
<tr><td>Monday 27</td></tr>
<tr><td>Tuesday 28</td></tr>
<tr><td>Wednesday 29</td></tr>
<tr><td>Thursday 30</td></tr>
</table>

Friday 31

Saturday 1

Sunday 2

Goals: _______________________________________

____

____

____

____

____

December

Su	Mo	Tu	We	Th	Fr	Sa
			1	2	3	4
5	6	7	8	9	10	11
12	13	14	15	16	17	18
19	20	21	22	23	24	25
26	27	28	29	30	31	

Activities

Date	Activity	Cost

Activities

Date	Activity	Cost

Activities

Date	Activity	Cost

Activities

Date	Activity	Cost

Activities

Date	Activity	Cost

Date	Activity	Cost

Activities

Date	Activity	Cost